KNOCK KNOCK JOKE BOOK FOR KIDS

Sheryl Green

MONKEY PUBLISHING

OUR HAND-PICKED
BOOK SELECTION FOR YOU.

LEARN
SOMETHING NEW
EVERYDAY.

ISBN: 9798501086869

Knock Knock .

Who's there?

Defense.

Defense who?

Defense has a hole in it—so our dog got loose.

Knock Knock

Who's there?

Sam

Sam who?

Sam person who knocked on the door last time!

Knock Knock

Who's there?

Elsie

Elsie who?

Elsie you later.

Knock Knock

Who's there?

Arfur

Arfur who?

Arfur got.

Knock Knock

Who's there?

Beef

Beef who?

Beef fair now!

Knock Knock

Who's there?

Abe.

Abe who?

Abe CDEFGH...

Knock Knock

Who's there?

Tim

Tim who?

Tim to go home.

Knock Knock

Who's there?

Wedding

Wedding who?

Wedding my pants, that's hilarious.

Knock Knock

Who's there?

Tamara.

Tamara who?

Tamara we'll be having tons of leftovers.

Knock Knock

Who's there?

Eddie.

Eddie who?

Eddie body get ready, it's time to go!

Knock Knock

Who's there?

Cereal

Cereal who?

Cereal pleasure to meet you!

Knock Knock

Who's there?

Mary.

Mary who?

Mary Christmas.

Knock Knock

Who's there?

Hal.

Hal who?

Hal will you know if you don't open the door?

Knock Knock

Who's there?

Ken

Ken who?

Ken I bring my dog to your house?

Knock Knock

Who's there?

Nose.

Nose who?

I nose plenty more knock-knock jokes!

Knock Knock

Who's there?

Norma Lee

Norme Lee who?

Norma Lee I have my key, can you let me in?

Knock Knock

Who's there?

Bella

Bella who?

Bella button.

Knock Knock

Who's there?

Howl.

Howl who?

Howl you know if you don't open the door?

Knock Knock.

Who's there?

Iran.

Iran who?

Iran over here to tell you this!

Knock Knock

Who's there?

Hugo

Hugo who?

Hugo first.

Knock Knock

Who's there?

Andrew!

Andrew who?

Andrew a picture!

Knock Knock

Who's there?

Aunt

Aunt who?

Aunt you glad I came?

Knock Knock

Who's there?

Tiss.

Tiss who?

Tiss who is good for blowing your nose.

Knock Knock

Who's there?

A little old lady.

A little old lady who?

Hey, you can yodel!

Knock Knock

Who's there?

Cargo.

Cargo who?

No, car go "beep beep"!

Knock Knock

Who's there?

Needle.

Needle who?

Needle little help getting in the door!

Knock Knock

Who's there?

Turnip.

Turnip who?

Turnip the volume. I love this song!

Knock Knock

Who's there?

Allison

Allison who?

Allison to the radio every morning!

Knock Knock

Who's there?

Eyesore.

Eyesore who?

Eyesore do love you!

Knock Knock

Who's there?

Hugh

Hugh who?

Hugh are nice!

Knock Knock

Who's there?

Snow.

Snow who?

Snow use. I forgot my name again!

Knock Knock .

Who's there?

Figs.

Figs who?

Figs the doorbell, it's not working!

Knock Knock

Who's there?

Dot

Dot who?

Dot com.

Knock Knock

Who's there?

Ron

Ron who?

Ron, Ron as fast as you can

Knock Knock

Who's there?

Annie.

Annie who?

Annie way you can let me in?

Knock Knock

Who's there?

Haden

Haden who?

Haden go seek.

Knock Knock

Who's there?

Lemon

Lemon who?

Lemon know when dinner is ready.

Knock Knock

Who's there?

Nobel.

Nobel who?

Nobel...that's why I knocked!

Knock Knock

Who's there?

Goat.

Goat who?

Goat to the door and find out.

Knock Knock

Who's there?

Omar

Omar who?

Omar goodness, I forgot my key!

Knock Knock

Who's there?

Mustache.

Mustache who?

Mustache you a question, but I'll shave it for later.

Knock Knock

Who's there?

Kiwi

Kiwi who?

Kiwi go to the store.

Knock Knock

Who's there?

Dina

Dina who?

Dina's ready, set the table

Knock Knock

Who's there?

Ivan

Ivan who?

Ivan the game!

Knock Knock

Who's there?

Dishes.

Dishes who?

Dishes a nice place you got here.

Knock Knock

Who's there?

Apollo

Apollo who?

I Apollo-gize, wrong door.

Knock Knock

Who's there?

Wendy.

Wendy who?

Wendy bell works again I won't have to

knock any more.

Knock Knock

Who's there?

Warrior

Warrior who?

Warrior been? I've been looking for you.

Knock Knock

Who's there?

Harry.

Harry who?

Harry up! It's cold out here!

Knock Knock.

Who's there?

Nana.

Nana who?

Nana your business.

Knock Knock

Who's there?

Bernardette

Bernardette who?

Bernadette all my dinner and now I'm starving!

Knock Knock

Who's there?

Beats

Beats who?

Beats me.

Knock Knock

Who's there?

X

X who?

X for breakfast.

Knock Knock

Who's there?

Aldo

Aldo who?

Aldo anything for you.

Knock Knock.

Who's there?

Howard.

Howard who?

Howard you like to sing Christmas carols with me?

Knock Knock

Who's there?

Adore

Adore who?

A door stands between us, open up!

Knock Knock

Who's there?

Ohio

Ohio who?

Ohio are you doing?

Knock Knock

Who's there?

Sue

Sue who?

Sue-prize!

Knock Knock

Who's there?

Alaska

Alaska who?

Alaska another question now...

Knock Knock

Who's there?

Harry

Harry who?

Harry armpits.

Knock Knock

Who's there?

Bless

Bless who?

I didn't sneeze!

Knock Knock

Who's there?

Dinosaur

Dinosaur who?

Dinosaurs don't go who, they go ROAR!

Knock Knock

Who's there?

Aaron.

Aaron who?

Why Aaron you opening the door?

Knock Knock.

Who's there?

Matt.

Matt who?

That's my full name, but my friends call me Matt.

Knock Knock

Who's there?

Dewey

Dewey who?

Dewey have to keep telling silly jokes?

Knock Knock

Who's there?

Ears.

Ears who?

Ears another knock knock joke for you!

Knock Knock

Who's there?

Wire.

Wire who?

Wire you always asking 'who's there'?

Knock Knock

Who's there?

Greta

Greta who?

Greta minds think alike.

Knock Knock

Who's there?

Roach

Roach who?

Roach you a letter, did you get it?

Knock Knock

Who's there?

Police.

Police who?

Police hurry up; it's chilly outside!

Knock Knock

Who's there?

Isabel.

Isabel who?

Isabel working? I had to knock!

Knock Knock

Who's there?

Howie

Howie who?

Howie doing today?

Knock Knock

Who's there?

Justin

Justin who?

Justin time for dinner.

Knock Knock

Who's there?

Claire.

Claire who?

Claire the way; I'm coming in!

Knock Knock.

Who's there?

Egg.

Egg who?

Eggstremely disappointed you still don't recognize me.

Knock Knock

Who's there?

Iowa

Iowa who?

Iowa big apology to you.

Knock Knock

Who's there?

Watson

Watson who?

Watson the table?

Knock Knock

Who's there?

Iva.

Iva who?

I've a sore hand from knocking!

Knock Knock

Who's there?

Doris.

Doris who?

Door is locked, that's why I'm knocking!

Knock Knock

Who's there?

Ashley

Ashley who?

Ashley, I don't really know.

Knock Knock

Who's there?

Ferdie

Ferdie who?

Ferdie last time, it's me!

Knock Knock

Who's there?

Amish

Amish who?

Really, you're a shoe?

Knock Knock

Who's there?

Echo

Echo who?

Echo who? Echo who?

Knock Knock

Who's there?

Closure.

Closure who?

Closure mouth while you're chewing!

Knock Knock

Who's there?

Chickens.

Chickens who?

Wrong, silly. Owls hoo. Chickens cluck.

Knock Knock

Who's there?

A herd.

A herd who?

A herd you were home, so I came over!

Knock Knock

Who's there?

Hair

Hair who?

Hair today, tomorrow who knows?

Knock Knock

Who's there?

Shelby

Shelby who?

Shelby home for Christmas

Knock Knock

Who's there?

Double.

Double who?

W.

Knock Knock

Who's there?

Justin.

Justin who?

Justin the neighborhood and thought I'd come over!

Knock Knock

Who's there?

Bean

Bean who?

Bean here for ages! What's taking you so long?

Knock Knock

Who's there?

You

You who?

Did you call me?

Knock Knock

Who's there?

Cow says.

Cow says who?

No, a cow says mooooo!

Knock Knock

Who's there?

Ben

Ben who?

Ben knocking for ages let me in.

Knock Knock

Who's there?

Sherlock.

Sherlock who?

Sherlock your door tight.

Knock Knock

Who's there?

Brad

Brad who?

Brad and butter.

Knock Knock

Who's there?

Tank.

Tank who?

You're welcome.

Knock Knock

Who's there?

Fozzie

Fozzie who?

Fozzie hundredth time let me in!

Knock Knock .

Who's there?

Chick.

Chick who?

Chick your stove, I can smell burning!

Knock Knock

Who's there?

Wooden shoe.

Wooden shoe who?

Wooden shoe like to hear another joke?

Knock Knock

Who's there?

Lettuce

Lettuce who?

Lettuce in, it's cold out here!

Knock Knock

Who's there?

Ezra

Ezra who?

Ezra anybody home?

Knock Knock

Who's there?

Cain

Cain who?

Cain you see me?

Knock Knock

Who's there?

Want.

Want who?

Want, who ... three, four, five!

Knock Knock

Who's there?

Tyrone.

Tyrone who?

Tyrone shoelaces!

Knock Knock

Who's there?

Lena

Lena who?

Lena a little closer, and I'll tell you another joke!

Knock Knock

Who's there?

Berry

Berry who?

Berry nice to meet you. Can I come in now?

Knock Knock

Who's there?

Honeydew.

Honeydew who?

Honeydew you want to hear some garden jokes?

Knock Knock

Who's there?

Zippy

Zippy who?

Mrs. Zippy.

Knock Knock

Who's there?

Ketchup

Ketchup who?

Ketchup later!

Knock Knock

Who's there?

Agatha

Agatha who?

Agatha go.

Knock Knock

Who's there?

Amos

Amos who?

A mosquito bit me!

Knock Knock

Who's there?

Mason

Mason who?

Mason, my wife and me.

Knock Knock

Who's there?

Cook.

Cook who?

Yeah, you do sound crazy!

Knock Knock

Who's there?

No one.

No one who?

Remains silent

Knock Knock

Who's there?

Alpaca.

Alpaca who?

Alpaca your lunch for school.

Knock Knock

Who's there?

Colin

Colin who?

Colin the police!

Knock Knock

Who's there?

Dwayne

Dwayne who?

Dwayne the bathtub. It is overflowing.

Knock Knock

Who's there?

Yule log.

Yule log who?

Yule log the door after you let me in, won't you?

Knock Knock

Who's there?

Avenue.

Avenue who?

Avenue knocked on this door before?

Knock Knock

Who's there?

Olive.

Olive who?

Olive you.

Knock Knock

Who's there?

Luke.

Luke who?

Luke through the peep hole and find out.

Knock Knock

Who's there?

Hawaii.

Hawaii who?

I'm fine, Hawaii you?

Knock Knock

Who's there?

Taco.

Taco who?

Taco to you later. It's taking too long for you to open the door.

Knock Knock

Who's there?

Aida.

Aida who?

Aida sandwich for lunch today.

Knock Knock

Who's there?

Laura

Laura who?

Laura the music, you'll wake up the neighbours

Knock Knock

Who's there?

Donut.

Donut who?

Donut ask, it's a secret!

Knock Knock

Who's there?

Beth

Beth who?

Beth bet is to open the door and find out!

Knock Knock

Who's there?

Maura

Maura who?

Maura less.

Knock Knock

Who's there?

Ida

Ida who?

Ida like to be your friend!

Knock Knock

Who's there?

Tennis

Tennis who?

Tennis five plus five

Knock Knock

Who's there?

Razor

Razor who?

Razor hand and dance the boogie!

Knock Knock

Who's there?

Mabel

Mabel who?

Mabel syrup!

Knock Knock

Who's there?

Toucan

Toucan who?

Toucan play this game!

Knock Knock

Who's there?

Iguana

Iguana who?

Iguana hold your hand

Knock Knock

Who's there?

Icing.

Icing who?

Icing so loud, the neighbors can hear.

Knock Knock

Who's there?

Butter.

Butter who?

Butter open the door. It's hot out here and I'm

melting.

Knock Knock

Who's there?

Jerrold

Jerrold who?

Jerrold friend, that's who!

Knock Knock

Who's there?

Diploma

Diploma who?

Diploma is here to fix the pipes.

Knock Knock

Who's there?

Heidi.

Heidi who?

Heidi 'cided to come over to play!

Knock Knock

Who's there?

Oink oink.

Oink oink who?

Make up your mind—are you a pig, or an owl?!

Knock Knock

Who's there?

Ya

Ya who?

I didn't know you were a cowboy!

Knock Knock

Who's there?

Woo.

Woo who?

Glad you're excited, too!

Knock Knock

Who's there?

Peas

Peas who?

Peas let me in.

Knock Knock

Who's there?

Yukon.

Yukon who?

Yukon say that again!

Knock Knock

Who's there?

Athena

Athena who?

Athena a ghost!

Knock Knock

Who's there?

Kent

Kent who?

Kent you tell by my voice?

Knock Knock

Who's there?

Nathan

Nathan who?

Nathan but the best for you.

Knock Knock

Who's there?

Otto

Otto who?

Otto know by now

Knock Knock

Who's there?

Keith

Keith who?

Keith me, my thweet prince!

Knock Knock

Who's there?

Althea

Althea who?

Althea later alligator.

Knock Knock

Who's there?

Sacha

Sacha who?

Sacha fuss, just because I knocked on your door?

Knock Knock

Who's there?

Misty

Misty who?

Misty bus, would you give me a ride?

Knock Knock

Who's there?

Hans

Hans who?

Hans off my Easter candy!

Knock Knock

Who's there?

LB

LB who?

LB seeing you!

Knock Knock

Who's there?

Watts.

Watts who?

Watts for dinner? I'm hungry.

Knock Knock

Who's there?

Impatient cow.

Impatient co...

MOO!

Knock Knock

Who's there?

Bee.

Bee who?

Bee-ware! All the ghosts are out on Halloween!

Knock Knock

Who's there?

Gary

Gary who?

Gary on smiling.

Knock Knock

Who's there?

Says.

Says who?

Says me!

Knock Knock

Who's there?

Will.

Will who?

Will you open the door?

Knock Knock

Who's there?

Caesar

Caesar who?

Caesars can help you cut things.

Knock Knock

Who's there?

Don

Don who?

Don talk back!

Knock Knock

Who's there?

Gladys.

Gladys, who?

Gladys the weekend—no homework!

Knock Knock

Who's there?

Mikey.

Mikey who?

Mikey doesn't fit in the key hole!

Knock Knock

Who's there?

Water.

Water who?

Water you doing? Just open the door!

Knock Knock

Who's there?

Repeat

Repeat who?

Who, who, who...

Knock Knock

Who's there?

Esther

Esther who?

Esther eggs!

Knock Knock

Who's there?

Philip

Philip who?

Philip my glass, please.

Knock Knock

Who's there?

John

John who?

John hands and make a circle.

Knock Knock

Who's there?

Scott

Scott who?

Scott nothing to do with you.

Knock Knock

Who's there?

Owls say.

Owls say who?

Yes, they do.

Knock Knock

Who's there?

Spain

Spain who?

Spain to have to keep knocking on this door!

Knock Knock

Who's there?

Utah.

Utah who?

U tal-king to me?

Knock Knock

Who's there?

Ice cream.

Ice cream who?

Ice cream if you don't let me in!

Knock Knock

Who's there?

Europe.

Europe who?

No, you're a pooh.

Knock Knock

Who's there?

Cher

Cher who?

Cher would be nice if you opened the door!

Knock Knock

Who's there?

CD.

CD who?

CD kid on your doorstep?

Knock Knock

Who's there?

Amy

Amy who?

Amy afraid I've forgotten.

Knock Knock

Who's there?

Abby.

Abby who?

Abby birthday to you!

Knock Knock

Who's there?

Anita

Anita who?

Anita borrow a piece of paper.

Knock Knock

Who's there?

Gorilla.

Gorilla who?

Gorilla me a hamburger.

Knock Knock

Who's there?

Dozen.

Dozen who?

Dozen anybody want to let me in?!

Knock Knock.

Who's there?

Cheese.

Cheese who?

Cheese a nice girl.

Knock Knock

Who's there?

Pisa

Pisa who?

Pisa cake.

Knock Knock

Who's there?

Esme

Esme who?

Esme tea ready yet?

Knock Knock

Who's there?

Hatch

Hatch who?

God bless you!

Knock Knock

Who's there?

Two knee.

Two knee who?

Two knee fish!

Knock Knock

Who's there?

Poodle

Poodle who?

Poodle little mustard on my hot dog, please.

Knock Knock

Who's there?

Rida

Rida who?

Rida lot of books!

Knock Knock

Who's there?

Tennessee

Tennessee who?

Tennessee played at Wimbledon!

Knock Knock.

Who's there?

Noah.

Noah who?

Noah anyone who can open this door?

Knock Knock

Who's there?

Tuna

Tuna who?

Tuna the piano and play me a song.

Knock Knock

Who's there?

Clara

Clara who?

Clara space on the table.

Knock Knock

Who's there?

Arbus

Arbus who?

Arbus leaves in 5 minutes.

Knock Knock

Who's there?

Goose

Goose who?

Goose who's knocking.

Knock Knock

Who's there?

Enoch

Enoch who?

Enoch and Enoch, but no one answers the door.

Knock Knock

Who's there?

Avery

Avery who?

Avery nice person. May I come in, please?

Knock Knock

Who's there?

Wanda.

Wanda who?

Wanda go watch the football game?

Knock Knock

Who's there?

Yellow

Yellow who?

Yellow, my name is Jamie.

Knock Knock

Who's there?

Mae

Mae who?

Mae be I'll tell you. Mae be I won't.

Knock Knock

Who's there?

Sid

Sid who?

Sid down.

Knock Knock

Who's there?

Radio.

Radio who?

Radi-o not, here I come.

Knock Knock

Who's there?

Norway

Norway who?

Norway I'm leaving.

Knock Knock

Who's there?

Witches.

Witches who?

Witches the way to the haunted cemetery?

Knock Knock

Who's there?

Karen

Karen who?

Karen heavy boxes, can you help me?

Knock Knock

Who's there?

Rufus

Rufus who?

Rufus leaking, and I'm getting wet.

Knock Knock

Who's there?

Kip

Kip who?

Kip out!

Knock Knock

Who's there?

Abby

Abby who?

Abby just stung me.

Knock Knock

Who's there?

Chicken

Chicken who?

Chicken your pockets if you can't find your keys.

Knock Knock

Who's there?

Goliath.

Goliath who?

Goliath down, you look tired!

Knock Knock

Who's there?

Carrie

Carrie who?

Carry me home, please.

Knock Knock

Who's there?

Oslo.

Oslo who?

Oslo down, what's the hurry!?

Knock Knock

Who's there?

Don

Don who?

Don be silly, you know who it is!

Knock Knock

Who's there?

Alec

Alec who?

Alec ice cream, don't you?

Knock Knock

Who's there?

Raichu

Raichu who?

Raichu are!

Knock Knock

Who's there?

Scold

Scold who?

Scold outside!

Knock Knock

Who's there?

Dennis

Dennis who?

Dennis took out my tooth.

Knock Knock

Who's there?

Alex

Alex who?

Alex-plain when you open the door!

Knock Knock

Who's there?

Kanga.

Kanga who?

I believe it is pronounced kanga-roo.

Knock Knock

Who's there?

Raina

Raina who?

Raina check.

Knock Knock

Who's there?

Art

Art who?

R2-D2!

Knock Knock

Who's there?

Igor

Igor who?

Igor to tell you something.

Knock Knock

Who's there?

Homer

Homer who?

Homer's where the heart is.

Knock Knock

Who's there?

Tunis

Tunis who?

Tunis company, three is a crowd.

Knock Knock

Who's there?

Annie.

Annie who?

Annie thing you can do, I can do too!

Knock Knock

Who's there?

Toby

Toby who?

Toby or not Toby, that's the question.

Knock Knock

Who's there?

Alvie

Alvie who?

Alvie back.

Knock Knock

Who's there?

Hope.

Hope who?

Hope you had a nice Christmas!

Knock Knock

Who's there?

Rhonda

Rhonda who?

Rhonda race!

Knock Knock

Who's there?

Chelsea

Chelsea who?

Chelsea for yourself when you open the door.

Knock Knock

Who's there?

Zany.

Zany who?

Zany body home?

Knock Knock

Who's there?

Isadore

Isadore who?

Isadore locked? I can't get in!

Knock Knock

Who's there?

Lionel

Lionel who?

Lionel bite you if you put your head in its mouth.

Knock Knock

Who's there?

Canoe.

Canoe who?

Canoe come out and play with me?

Knock Knock

Who's there?

Spell.

Spell who?

W. H. O.

Knock Knock

Who's there?

Weekend.

Weekend who?

Weekend do anything we want.

Knock Knock

Who's there?

Carlos

Carlos who?

Carlos his umbrella, do you have a spare?

Knock Knock

Who's there?

Pecan!

Pecan who?

Pecan somebody your own size!

Knock Knock

Who's there?

Jaws

Jaws who?

Jaws truly.

Knock Knock

Who's there?

Tokyo

Tokyo who?

What Tokyo so long to open the door.

Knock Knock

Who's there?

Xena

Xena who?

Xena good movie lately?

Knock Knock

Who's there?

Carl.

Carl who?

Car'll get you there faster than a bike.

Knock Knock

Who's there?

Two knee.

Two knee who?

Two knee your piano, and it'll sound better.

Knock Knock

Who's there?

Orange.

Orange who?

Orange you glad to see me?

Knock Knock

Who's There?

Barbie

Barbie Who?

Barbie Q Chicken.

Knock Knock

Who's there?

Candice

Candice who?

Candice joke get any worse?!

Knock Knock

Who's there?

Irish.

Irish who?

Irish you a Merry Christmas!

Knock Knock

Who's there?

Howard

Howard who?

I'm fine, Howard you?

Knock Knock

Who's there?

Mice

Mice who?

Mice to meet you.

Made in the USA
Columbia, SC
25 November 2021

49570350R00064